Later in the Mourning

LATER
IN THE
MOURNING

Daph Willett

Later in the Mourning
Daph Willett

Published by Aspect Design 2018
Malvern, Worcestershire, United Kingdom.

Designed, printed and bound by Aspect Design
89 Newtown Road, Malvern, Worcs. WR14 1PD
United Kingdom
Tel: 01684 561567
E-mail: allan@aspect-design.net
Website: www.aspect-design.net

Artwork by Roy Willett, Daph Willett and Kelvin Willsher

Cover Design Copyright © 2018 Aspect Design

ISBN 978-1-909219-53-3

*My thanks to Karen Doyle for my treatments
and much listening and friendship ongoing.*

To Nina Shields for her continued 'clarity' of thinking

*To Dave and Beryl Eserin for continuing
care and practical help, so valued.*

*Deep appreciation to Bridget Walker for her
empathy and care for Roy and myself
as she walks the losses of her own grief.*

To Iris Print for their printing and patience.

To Aspect Design for their valued expertise.

Continued love and strength to Kelvin, who is still working with multiple losses so early in his life. Also his continued support for me.

In respect of loss and grief's
Journey, and some of its stages,
And its memories of those –
Our family lost – to which many may relate!

Later in the Mourning

Though you do not see me weep,
   My heart it cries, its silent tears.
How could it not the deepness feel?
   For you were with me—'Tens of Years'.

Introduction

This lengthy path of grieving is different for everyone; each person needs to feel it and work through it their own way. Some may progress sooner than others, each person's journey is their own.

The early days of grief are busy and demanding, with legalities, formalities and duties. Grieving takes second place. As the duties come to their completion, the real depth of the loss surfaces.

Anger, sorrow and longing vie inside us day by day. You ebb and flow like an ever-changing tide.

'This is so normal.'

'This is so scary.'

Time can only distance you from your day of loss, it is not a healer. When those you love die, a part of you dies with them. The loss is always there, just below the surface–you don't get over this, you just learn to live beside it. If you can face it, which is not easy, you slowly learn to cope.

It's good to talk about it with someone. Take courage—take time to feel and learn about your grief and yourself. Seek help, if it helps you to share. Nothing will totally heal the part where you held the ones love.

Time allows the wretchedness to be come more controlled. With time—slowly—you *do* learn to cope.

Remember the good times you shared with those you've lost. Celebrate them inside yourself, it will help you to cope.

'Be kind to yourself.'

In Time

Deep and quiet remains my grief,
    To break in silver shards.
When something touches memory,
    Sweet music or a card.

But I can hold it now within,
    So only I will know,
Then, if I'm in safe company,
    My silver shards, I'll show.

No Less Love

No less love.
No less pain.
No less sorrow.
But always loved
And always missed,
Through every next tomorrow.

Now turn that love inside you,
As they would want you to.
Feel their warmth surround you
In everything you do.

This is no rapid journey.
Grief's road is filled with pain.
So let their love enfold you,
Again—again—and again.

To Memory

The love is secure
  My heart is still true.
The year's quickly pass,
  Since the loss of you.

The unity of love and care,
  Is stronger e'en than death.
It still brings me comfort through my days
  With each and every breath

If Only

Can you catch my falling tears,
And thread them in a row?
Can you hold my sparkling gems,
So only you can know?

Could you hold my fragile heart,
So no one else can break it?
Could you there in worlds apart
To dwell with you—please take it?

Can you warm my frozen soul,
That bides on earth alone.
Can you guide and nurture it,
Till my soul and me, come home?

Changes

The shape of life,
Has changed forever,
Since you slipped away.
The flame of love still brightly burns
And flickers gently as it turns,
Inward, to where it often yearns,
As I live another day.

Loss is like a steep, steep hill,
You climb awhile, and pause.
You couldn't do it in one go,
And progress is so very slow.
But some way on it, you will know,
It's for your own good cause.

Each time you pause, each time you yearn,
Your soul will come to know,
That your presence now is here, inside.
It comforts, deep, where you now abide,
I hold you there with love and pride,
Which creates an inner glow.

Reaching Out

The shrouded mists
That form the veil,
Between your world and mine.
Can I, with love,
Pass through that mist,
And link our souls to shine?

Could that measured comfort bring,
To warm my endless days?
Could that love to you extend.
In a million different ways?
Could your dear soul, in peace then thrive?
Then I, myself, can strengthened be, now I alone survive.

Losing a Child

To dear Bridget, for the loss of her daughter, Abbey

The vibrance of your lively soul.
The care its rhythm brings.
I still feel it in my heart,
As in each beat it rings.
It was always linked to music,
And also linked in words,
They still vibrate inside me
And a harmony records,
The great peace of my emotion,
Your essences afford.

Those visual pictures that were made,
Are just our outer bind.
The complimentary sharing
Of ingenuity, and mind.

On this transcendental journey
That links both hearts and minds.
With pen or paint on paper,
Your 'stage presence', so defined.

It's always there, though now you've gone,
To sustain me on life's way.
Thank you for your precious gifts.
They encourage me every day.

You were a very special child,
Your talents left for me to see.
I am so very proud to know,
That you came to earth—through me.
I couldn't know, when you were born,
The journey we would share.
I hope your soul has founds its peace,
With our tender, loving care.

Struggling Still with Child Loss

Untie for me this tangled way,
Whose mists have shadowed my direction.
Unlock for me the hidden door,
So I may escape my insurrection.

The loss of you was so unfair.
Your shattered life unreal.
Your vibrance severed in a trice,
What am I 'supposed' to feel?

Your ingenuity so sadly passed,
And you are here no more.
Parting is still such a sorrow,
Deep in my innermost core.

Child Loss Reflection

Oh you dearest child of mine,
    Whose time on Earth is spent.
And from that day as of your birth.
    Your life to us was lent.

Did you know your valued soul,
    Had precious work to do?
To labour here, to make it whole,
    So you could make it through.

And we were but the catalyst,
    To guide you on your way.
And for such a touching honour,
    We say thank you every day.

Remembering

I feel still your presence here.
I still miss your cheerful smile.
That deeply held much meaning,
'for that special while.'

In the depth of love we shared.
In that smile, I know you cared.
In our life, your heart you bared,
'In that special while.'

'Thank you.'

Contemplation

Come quieten now my weeping soul,
  So I can feel you near today.
Your place was here beside me,
  And then you went away.

I'm working hard to weather this.
  Though still I'm not sure how.
Slowly through the mist of tears,
  More peace is growing now.

I know your love is with me,
  I feel you always there,
On this the strangest journey,
  With no one now to share.

To My Child

I hear the spirit of the wind,
　　Whispering your name.
The sensual spirit of the hare,
　　Doing just the same.
The whole of nature's messengers,
　　Seem to have you in their frame.

The times we shared fly back to me,
　　The memories now aflame.
So I am strengthened through my day
　　Knowing you are still the same.
Then I will shed my tears for you,
　　On my lowest darkest plain.

This is the pathway of my grief.
　　To feel it all and sense the pain.
Every step a lesson here,
　　To experience now, and yet again.
So find peace in your own value here,
　　Then your 'child' can do the same.

A Lost Child

In the beauty of the memories that are him.
In the sorrow at his death, that is mine.
In the peace of the knowledge that he lives,
In the lives of us for all time.

In the hearts of the suffering be there peace.
In the comfort of knowing—someone's there.
In the darkest moments among sorrows.
In the depth of our deepest despair.

In the quiet of our souls is a stirring.
In the love that is shown to us all.
In the care that will always surround us.
In the people who hear when we call.

In the faces of friends there is caring.
In the music of life as it flows.
In the hours when we all 'struggle forward'.
In ourselves, as again our faith grows.

Listen

Did I hear your voice just then?
　　I thought I heard you call.
I know I felt your warmth around.
　　But there was no sound at all,
My room, it just felt warmer.
　　My thoughts had turned to you.
I'm sure you touched my shoulder,
　　Just like you used to do.

The pleasure of that feeling,
　　Lightened up my day
It lifted up my spirit,
　　As if you'd come to stay.
They said that this might happen,
　　That it would come in time.
They said your love would penetrate,
From your world into mine.

Somewhere

Somewhere on a distant shore,
    I hope you've found your peace.
Your fights and fears are over and
Your victory established,
    So your soul may earn release.

Can I reach out and touch you?
    If I knew now, where you are.
If I could only find you,
    My own elusive star.

The time now passes quickly.
    The winter ghosts are here.
The grey skies lock the heavens,
    As the winter holds no cheer.

Where do I stand in this new life?
    The tick of time flicks quickly by.
I need to reconstruct my world,
    And a brand new purpose try.

Soon the spring will break the shards
    Of winter's deeps, and show,
All nature's hope around me.
    Empowering me to grow.

I hear the distant future call.
    Now I must make my way,
Upon this long and rocky road,
To a goal that's ever nearer now,
    Each and every day.

Realisation

A million waves have kissed the shore,
As years slip by, a million more,
Will break and crash in nature's way.
It is a pattern, day by day.

Tinselled fish float in morning sun.
People and dogs on the shore will run.
Children dance and laugh before,
New patterns develop again, once more.

This is the passing of real time.
This is what I need to find.
This I've mislaid since I lost you,
And redirecting I must do.

In this my life, where am I going?
Years have passed without me knowing,
And grief and loss of our life together,
Bring sorrows long I have to weather.

Slowly as the time go by,
I've ceased to beg the question 'Why?'
Your being, is now deep inside my heart.
So my new journey I may start.

Malvern Memories

Take me to the Bluebell Wood.
    Please, Roy, please.
Its carpet of beauty calls me, and
    The quiet of its trees,
Enthral me, through my spirit,
    Its colours give my soul,
Peace, with man and nature, and it
    Makes my vision whole.

Be with me in the Bluebell Wood.
    Please, Roy, please.
The fragrant, peaceful memories
    Surround us in these trees.
Those minutes here in silence,
    Were many, and remain
So precious in our life's backdrop,
    That we shared—and would again.

There was peace amongst the bluebells.
    Remember, Roy, please.
Each tiny bell's a messenger
    Of purpose with the trees.
We stood entranced in quiet,
    Imbibing through the soul,
The perfectness of nature.
    That made both our spirits whole.

My Comfort

I think I felt you kiss my cheek.
    And brush my tears away.
To comfort me this morning,
    As I begin another day.

You raise my spirits on these days.
    When I turn to think of you.
Amid the hurt of separation,
    As again the pain comes through.

Now I've learned to feel you more,
    Deep in the chambers of my heart.
I begin to feel you frequently,
    Since I let the healing start.

It doesn't mean I don't still cry.
    I doesn't mean I'm 'through'.
    It doesn't mean I miss you less,
    In everything I do.

It means that on this 'no choice path'
    I falter, but will find my way.
I'll learn to talk with you inside,
    And I do that now, each day.

I feel now that you are with me.
    I hear the words you say.
I know your love is constant,
    In a warming, telepathic way.

Progress

I hold you here in memory.
    Long weeks have turned to years.
I've learned to face the world again,
    With slightly fewer tears.

I'll always long for yesterday,
    And want to feel your touch.
But I feel the surge within me now,
    And this becomes my crutch.

I value so our moments,
    That no one ever knew
When you'd whisper me your loving,
    And I'd do the same to you.

We grew it here together,
    It was our own real way.
I remember things you wrote to me,
    And beautiful things you'd say.

They live inside my heart now,
    And bring me peace at night
They steady me throughout my day.
    Now I know, I'll be alright.

New Masks

I see the people's faces,
    All around and know,
They think I'm back to normal.
    As my depth I do not show.

Having learned to laugh and act
    Like I know they want me to.
And yes, I enjoy a lot of it,
    Just enough to get me through.

This can't go on forever,
    I'm running out of masks.
My inner strength is waning
    As I cope with daily tasks.

Only if you've walked this path,
    Will you know what these words mean.
That your depth of changing sorrows,
    Have now to go unseen.

Unseen, but real and pertinent,
    The feelings that we hide.
Where the longing keeps on surfacing
    And the love, is held with pride.

Turning Point

So every heart to loss, shall come.
    Then every soul shall grieve.
Accumulated sorrows,
    Too many to believe.
Oh stand beside me through these times,
    And catch my tears by night.
So remnants of our love may heal,
    And show me there is light.

So I may feel the start of peace,
    And slowly come to know,
That to hold your love—inside me,
    Will light an inner glow.
I so need this transformation,
    From the emptiness of sorrow,
To give my soul a foothold,
    So to build a new tomorrow.

Thanks

You were a lighthouse in my life,
　　So I could see my way.
Your beams lit up my needing heart
　　And lit a brand new day.

That was so many years ago.
　　When both our hearts entwined,
And my lost heart was needing you,
　　And yours, was needing mine.

Now your light has dimmed away,
　　And I'm alone once more.
I still feel your warmth inside me
　　And it warms me to my core.

As this time for grief slips by
　　And its days have turned to years.
In my soul your light still shines,
　　Still calms, and holds my fears.

Thank you for your affirming.
　　The memories shine so bright.
They steady now my journey,
　　So thank you for the light.

The Shock

Deep in the chambers of my heart,
Locked inside my soul.
There's a dawning of tomorrow,
To find a fresh direction, so
Moving forward is the goal.

The time has fled and run away,
Since I was there for you.
I hold the truths in memory now
Of all the things we'd do.
I visualize them every day,
        just to get me through.

I'll never regret those times we shared,
Creativity, love and tears.
Then Alzheimers came to stay with us,
It was so depleting, so unkind.
It wiped away our years.

Grief comes knocking, as it wants
And holds you in its thrall.
It has no timely structure,
        so try to take control.
You need the strength of purpose now,
To follow your own goal.

Alzheimers

The one I loved had disappeared.
Long before his death.
I'm glad I was beside him,
Up to his final breath.
I came to be his safety,
Morning, noon and night.
That vibrant man I married,
Lost in his own plight.
You lose your own persona
When Alzheimers comes to stay.
But the depth of love in your soul place,
It can never take away.

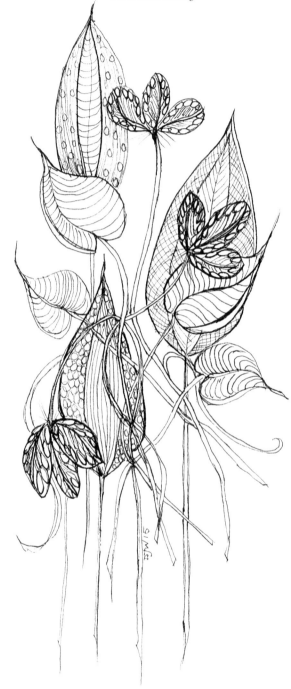

Recollections

The days when we were happy
　　So many now I cherish.
The mornings' helpless laughter,
　　That both of us could relish.
When you would offer up a word,
　　Which our humour would embellish.

Oh lovely, funny recollections
　　Exclusive to our life.
Lots of laughs and great selections,
　　That made me want to be your wife.
Then the word, 'Alzheimers',
　　Came here with us to dwell,
On the saddest journey.
　　Which for us all, was hell.

So who am I, now, the years have gone?
　　What now, my new direction?
So many years of caring done,
　　With no personal selection.
Now each day—the hours—are mine.
　　With only retrospection.

So live inside me now forever,
　　Like a warm and fragrant glow.
So I can feel your heart beat,
　　Just like you used to show.
Then I can take the comfort now
　　From everything I know.

Words

The words, oh the words.
The beautiful words,
They tumble, jumble,
Through your head.
They wake you through the tossing night hours,
Demanding loudly, to be said.

They pour out in streams a rushing,
From places you didn't know were there,
Too deep for knowledge in your day space,
In grief and sorrow that we share.
Longing stirs them up—all jumbled,
And the words, are jumbled up with care.

Our words—your words—'the' words.
We shared the love of words.
Calligraphic—written and unspoken,
Poetry for the soul
Cleansing, evocative, cathartic.
Satisfying and whole.

Spoken words, the Art of the Poet.
Poetry of the Artist, linking the conscious
To the sub consciousness of the soul.
The need to express, words well chosen,
To touch the heart and make the spirit whole.

The only thing left to give, is words

Thinking

Take time for contemplation.
    To slip inside, to feel and know,
And get to 'feel' your being.
    The parts you never show.

Allow yourself, reflection,
    Slow down your busy life.
Take some minutes everyday.
    Stand back from the stress and strife.

This will—'still'—your thinking,
    And allow your brain to 'slow'.
It will alter your decisions
    Of how you come and go.

It's a speck of satisfaction
    In your busy, busy day,
To hear your inner being,
    Having a little say.

The Heart

Every heart to grief will come,
    That grief, will grip your soul.
Everyone's own journey,
    In loss, will take its toll.
If acceptance of this state of mind,
    Is avoided, to extreme.
The hurt just dwells inside you,
    Then your living will demean.
Try to let some healing start,
    Look inside and see,
You and your soul are valuable,
    So have strength in what will be.
Face your loss, and feeling.
    Cry, or shout or moan.
Share with someone if you can,
    You don't have to be alone.

On Difficult Days

Like the wailing of the banshee,
   In the concentrated mind.
In the depth one cannot access,
   In the reasons one can't find.

The cacophony of losses,
   That penetrate the soul.
In the sound of one's own essences,
   That make a spirit whole.

So hold that essence in your sight.
   Nurture it and let it grow.
Hold on to value and your direction.
   Even if that journey's slow.

Time Lapse

Nearly two years now, have flown,
    Since I was by your side.
I suppose I'm coping now, as then,
    Holding my defences, as in the hour you died.
Slowly, contemplation calms the aching soul, and
    To carry you within me, will begin to make me whole.
You are still mine and I so need your role,
    Come steady now my pathway, as coping is my goal.

People said, grief's road was slow
    And there's nowhere here to hide,
I have to grieve at my own pace
    And to turn to you, inside.
Two hearts still there in memory, thus,
    Still with love entwine.
One of them is yours my love,
    And the other one, is mine.

Acknowledgement

Hear the words I say to you,
    Each and every night.
Hear the warmth of love they bring,
    With awareness of hindsight.

Now I know oh so much more,
    About you, and your deepest scar.
And can you feel my love tonight?
    It is where you are.

Your Sparkle

Oh sparkle for me in the sky,
　　When day has turned to night.
Oh show me where you are by day,
　　In every song bird's flight.
Touch my hand, when I touch the flowers,
　　So I may feel you're there.
All this may help my journey,
　　And reimburse your care.
I need this reassurance,
　　To transcend the deepest sorrows,
To know your love is with me,
　　Through all, my long tomorrows.

This Road

You don't have to like this journey,
    As on this road there's no selection.
It's about awareness of who you are,
    And about your new direction.

As every heart to grief will come,
    Then all will know this 'way'.
As time lapses into years on years,
    More structured grief comes in to play.

The life that was, has died with you.
    I'd still choose to taste some more.
Raw loss, it shows us many things,
    We didn't know before.

With knowledge understanding grows,
    So forgiveness too can come.
It brings more peace into your grief,
    Until your grieving's done.

Questions

Who am I now? I do not know.
So deep within, I'm striving so,
To find out who and why.

The soul, I gave so readily,
Has now been given back to me.
And I must work, and try.

To find a way that's right for me,
With willing spirit, as there must be,
A purpose for me here—I cry.

Which way to turn, now I'm alone,
Without that background, 'bass voice tone',
A scary time that I can't deny.

What has my God in mind for me,
I'm ready for the challenge now,
So show me and I'll try.

I have the warmth of one who's gone,
Whose deepest love protects within.
I so need that protection now,
     as a different life begins.

Rhythm

Can you feel the rhythm,
    That beats in everything?
It's in your steady heart beat,
    And in raging winds that bring,
    The persistent beating rainfall,
    And in the birds that sing.

It's present through your grieving,
    And how you weep, with tears.
It's in your contemplation,
    Which you need to steady fears.
It replicates your heart beat
    That helps your thoughts stay clear.

We need that simple rhythm,
    To steady every breath.
Its familiar, safe and structured,
    The body knows it best.
And if we're stressed and suffering,
    It bids you, take a rest.

Take courage now and forward look.
    Hear its beat beneath life's din.
It builds comforting expectancies,
    So your new life can begin.
It's in this little poem, on it you can rely.
Let your spirit move to it,
    so your body can comply.

Dilemma

How do you step back from the past?
How do you forward go?
Essences, from your lost one's love
Live in you now—you know.

This is calming, safe and special,
Emotional and fine.
But you can't just live within that sphere,
You must create another way.
A change is needed—that is clear,
To re-structure, every day.
There are thousands of us in this place,
Struggling with no choice,
Who've stemmed their lists of longing,
Souls, now waiting, for a voice.

Now

I know I feel your presence,
    I feel it more and more.
The comfort in its warming
    Penetrates me to my core.
The years we stood together,
    Are meaning so much more.

This journey isn't easy,
    It will always be the same.
I still miss your vibrant beauty
    And your senses all aflame.
Your wit, I hear inside me, and
    Your flippancy with no shame.

Now I know—I can go forward.
    Now I know—I'll be okay.
Now I know—that I shall make it,
    As you come to me each day.
Thank you for our lifetime
    As in my heart you stay.

Love

Love changes everything
 As the song believes.
This message so defining
 Allows us to retrieve,
Belief in our own sensuality,
 That is, 'forgotten' as we grieve.

It's still there, deep inside you,
 The sensual being, in your soul.
Hear your inner messages,
 Contemplate a goal.
Knowledge blossoms freely, and
 You need to take control.
As now inside, you're ready,
 To face another role.

Keep grounded

To Those Who Grieve

To anyone who reads this book
And who understands these words.
They must be treading grief's long track
And know 'there is no turning back'.
With empathy, I reach out to you.
I feel just where you're standing.
Persevere now on your path,
Though it's hard and so demanding.
Soon, some better days will come,
When the soul can sense a calming.
Hold on to your value, reinstate your being.
I wish you strength, as you find your way,
To a future peace, you're seeing.

Be kind to yourselves.

Feel Me

Feel me in your inmost soul
    As my heart with yours entwines.
Feel my love, protecting you,
    As each day we still combine.
Feel me in your thoughts today,
    Don't let my memory sever.
Feel me all around your world.
    Feel me in you, Forever.

My Wish For You

Weep, oh weep for me a little.
　　Grieve for me not a measured while.
As your life goes slowly onward,
　　Think of me, and raise a smile.
And soon, you'll smile much more than weep,
　　So peace may drop its dew.
　　To heal the space, where I once dwelt,
　　When I was there—with you.
Then inside my essence keep,
　　Open your soul and feel.
So I may live there every day,
　　And you'll always know—I'm real.

'The ties of love are eternal'

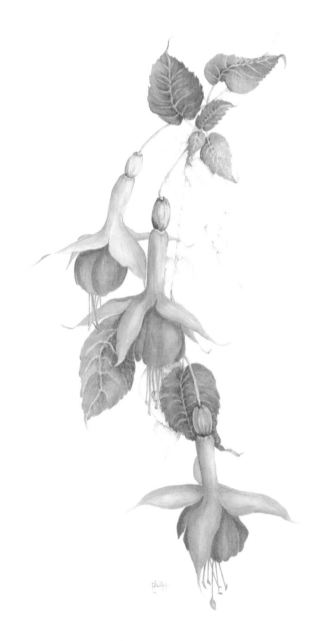

With empathy and care